Then God MADE A WOMAN

UNWRAPPING FEMALE SEXUALITY

NANCY HOUSTON

LICENSED PROFESSIONAL COUNSELOR
AND CERTIFIED SEX THERAPIST

Then God Made a Woman: Unwrapping Female Sexuality
Clear Wind Publishing

Copyright © 2023 by Nancy Houston

Manufactured in the United States of America

Library of Congress Cataloging-in-Publication Data is available.
ISBN: 979-8-218-15203-1

CONTENTS

	Introduction	1
1.	Sexuality	9
2.	Intentional Design	13
3.	Female Sexual Anatomy	21
4.	Liberating View of Sexuality	27
5.	Sexual History	31
6.	Sexuality for Singles	35
7.	Sexuality for Married Women	43
8.	Sex: God's Idea	49
9.	Feeling Safe	55
10.	Understanding Female and Male Sexual Differences	59
11.	Sex is Her Choice	63
12.	Happy Married Sex	73
13.	You Are Resilient	81
	Notes	85

Dedication

For Ron

To the man I have loved for nearly fifty years.

Your steady love has provided a safe haven for me to

become *me*.

You are a gift, and I adore you.

INTRODUCTION

I t's the dead of winter. The sky is gray, and my swimming pool has ringlets from raindrops falling. Mostly my plants are greenish brown, yet, from the brown vines climbing my arbor, three little sunshine blossoms shaped like trumpets pop their heads out against the backdrop. Our sexuality can appear much like those three yellow blossoms cautiously asking, "Can we blossom though it's the dead of winter?" Yes, and yes! Permission given for you, as a woman, to blossom despite the season or the circumstances of your life—blossom is what you shall do. Like petals opening and releasing fragrant perfume, so you were meant to allow your sexuality room to release, explore, be held, and appreciated.

We have had such a limited, little view of female sexuality, and silly ideas defined by those who are simply too afraid to acknowledge its depth, meaning, and beauty have been given the power to decide what female sexuality is and what it means. —No more.

The Song of Songs starts with the woman boldly saying, "Kiss me--full on the mouth! Yes! For your love is better than wine, headier than your aromatic oils." She knows the power of her desire and she owns it with a confidence that is appealing, not brash. Desire is to own the *want*.

Wait a minute; hold the phone. I have permission to own my want? My desires aren't inherently evil?

Nope—they aren't.

Scripture clearly says, "I will give you the desires of your heart."

Well, that's terrifying; you may think, *What if my desires are evil or wild or out of control?*

Our minds automatically go to some wild, out-of-control place when we think of desire. We momentarily visualize something outrageous or worse, doing something outrageous. Shame follows so we keep our desires under wraps: we fear them, we demonize them. So instead of being able to love with abandonment we keep the most magnificent part of ourselves under wraps.

But wait. Are your sexual desires outrageous?

Rarely do people actually want to live out their sexual fantasies. Mostly people want to have a loving, warm, healthy, and meaningful sexual relationship. My sexual desires lean toward the man I have loved for nearly 50 years. I'm like the Shulamite in the Song of Songs. I love his kisses, they still melt me, and I love the strength and warmth of his body. When we put our arms around each other, and I take a moment to breathe him in, my body relaxes. His quiet strength is what I take in. I put my ear to his chest and my nervous system calms and my muscles let go, as I hear the beating of his heart. I deepen my embrace of him and allow my desire to arise. There is something indescribable that happens. We have loved long enough and fought often enough to be at home with each other. Our bodies speak their own love language. Words aren't necessary. He is my desire. I say that unashamedly as I believe the Shulamite did as well. My desire for my husband is good. God said everything He made is good, and He made you sexual. He gave you a sexual nervous system when He wired you together in your mother's womb, and your body was designed to respond to sexual stimuli—it is good.

Sadly, we have focused mostly on what is bad and because of this fear-driven fact we have missed what is good. I'm not in denial, there is sexual bad. There is plenty of sexual bad, and the Bible talks bluntly about it. Stories of rape, incest, adultery, murder, abuse, and family sexual dysfunction vividly fill the pages of the Old Testament stories. God doesn't pretend humans haven't used what was meant to be good, beautiful, and sacred for bad and evil. No. He tells the truth and so must we. And yet we must equally hold on to the good. Sex is sacred and beautiful and there is nothing so lovely as to lay naked with the one you love, to be embraced and intertwined in one another's bodies. There is no greater nonverbal way of expressing love than the sharing of two bodies committed to marital bliss.

You may be protesting; *it isn't all bliss*: he comes too quickly; I can't keep up, he's so fast; I don't have time to even get warmed up; he crosses the finish line, and I haven't left the gate; he's full of sexual energy and I can't find the match;

Or . . .

When he was younger he seemed sexually insatiable, now he's conked out every night snoring and I feel sexually neglected; his erections aren't what they used to be, so he just seems to avoid the whole thing now; I don't want to get naked with him; I don't feel safe, he prefers looking at naked women on his computer; his affair has left me feeling empty, resentful, and cut off from him; I don't know how to find my way back to him; his children exhaust me.

These things feel hurtful and make those three little smiling blossoms of your sexuality want to close up tight and never come out, but I believe a significant part of adulting is to define yourself sexually and to free yourself from the pressures of the stories you have been told. Maybe you feel pressured to be sexy or funny or agreeable? Perhaps your partner pouts when they don't get sex and you feel responsible to regulate them emotionally? It's time to unburden yourself and decide who you are as a sexual creature. It's also time to integrate your spirituality with your sexuality. I would encourage every woman reading this book to invite God in to teach, affirm, and define who you are as a sexual creature.

Human sexuality is not simplistic—it is complex. But we humans don't like complex. That's why we tell teenagers and young adults to follow all the sexual rules the "sex police" have created and when you get married, you will have a sexual paradise. Imagine how disappointing that is to those who have been told this story over and over, only to get married and find out that sexuality and learning how to make love to another human takes time, willingness, desire, and being humble enough to allow the other person to teach us how they want to be touched? There is nothing simplistic about it.

Even though sexuality isn't simplistic, I believe it is a noble battle to be fought for and a treasure worthy of being sought after. Your sexuality is a gift from God. We cannot deny, ignore, or take for granted this beautiful gift, lest it die. God made you sexual for a purpose. He has a plan. Are you willing to discover and reclaim the beauty of this mysterious gift? If you are, then I invite you to move past your pride, hurt, and prejudices, and discover all God was saying when He made you a woman.

CHAPTER ONE

SEXUALITY

God intends for a created pattern of joy and mutuality in the ecstasy and fulfillment of intimacy in marital love between man and woman. God purposefully made women sexual. Like the Shulamite in the Song of Songs, it's time for us to cast off the old messages and to dance a dance of victory, snuffing out the old shameful beliefs about female sexuality and embracing God's beautiful design for us as women.

We can do this by speaking up, using our voices for the good of all, and supporting one another in seeking and believing in healthy sexuality for all humans. We can provide good help for people who have suffered from sexual trauma. We can stop blaming victims and start supporting them. We can be a voice for the voiceless by admitting there are perpetrators who need to serve jail time and women and children deserve to be protected from them. We can also believe that most men are good, and they too have been affected by unhealthy messages. We can band together and become the picture of male and female representing the goodness of God's creation.

God created women in His perfect design—not as an after-thought. Some theologians call women the crown of God's creation, the crescendo, the final astonishing work of the creator. Yet so many women have reported they don't like their bodies or their sexuality. Their bodies and sex have created lots of pain and shame, and many have learned how to separate themselves from their bodies, often starting at young ages. Girls frequently feel shame for developing into a female body because of the comments and leering, eventually believing they are only valued for their bodies.

This shaming of the female body can frequently lead to deep seated feelings of rejection. Dallas Willard said, "Western culture is, largely unbeknown to itself, a culture of rejection." When women are reduced to sexual objects or seen as either a threat or created to dutifully serve men's sexual desires, it affects their sense of dignity and self-regard. It is demeaning to all, both females and males.

What if we put away some of our false assumptions about female sexuality and explored the wonders of what God was saying through His unique design of women? Perhaps we would change some of our deeply held beliefs and wounding messages about females and hold them with a higher regard. I believe if we became more compassionate, kind, and curious with ourselves about our sexuality we could work through many, if not all, of our sexual issues.

I am saddened by the messages women have received from the Evangelical world. Yes, some are wonderful and healthy and pro female sexuality, but way too many are misusing scripture to communicate, whether purposefully or naively, that women were created as less than and are responsible to fulfill the sexual needs of men or are dangerous threats to male purity. These messages are not only counter to the teaching of the Bible, but counter to the Christ who loves us.

In scripture, every interaction Jesus has with a female is one of respect and looking beyond her circumstances to see the human with empathy, compassion, and respect. I believe it is time to unveil harmful unbiblical or extra-biblical sexual messages and replace them with a true biblical view of human sexuality—a view that elevates both males and females.

CHAPTER TWO

INTENTIONAL DESIGN

If we looked at what God was saying through creation and how He made female anatomy, we would be convinced God was saying female sexuality is meant to be a grand celebration; it is divine, holy, good, and purposeful. God decided female sexual pleasure was very significant and important to Him. Important enough that He would do a 2.0 when He created the female because females have double the potential for pleasure.

If all females, both married and single, had a greater understanding of the significance in which God created us, we would value ourselves more highly, with more respect and self-regard, we would understand our significance and the deep profound thoughtfulness God put into each one of us when He created us female. Many females suffer with body image issues and low self-regard, but if we took in all God was saying through the making of our bodies we could take hold of how wonderfully and marvelously we are made.

I suffered with body image and low self-regard because I grew up with a lot of trauma. I remember feeling as if I were a prisoner to my traumatic memories. A rape in high school by a youth pastor, not feeling safe in my childhood home, and sexual abuse from my father while my mother turned a blind eye and a deaf ear, left me feeling vulnerable, scared, ashamed, and alone. Prisons mostly take place in our minds, restraining us with invisible shackles. We give memory power by replaying it over and over or by holding it far away, in denial of the pain. Believing it will be too terrifying, we refuse to let the memory up and out. We get triggered and suddenly we are in two places, the present and the past.

The past can take over, and this is where we must learn to be compassionate to the part of us that holds these memories. We hold on to the adult part of ourselves. This is how you can process with the younger part of yourself holding the pain:

Say to this younger part:

"It's okay. I am here for you; I will hold you and help you through this. You are safe now. You can talk about what happened, and I will listen. I will stop judging you harshly. I will listen to your story. I will stay grounded and help you stay grounded. We will be okay. The past is over, and now is your time to heal; it's okay to ask for help. I will find a qualified sex therapist, who is trauma informed, and I will help you by being compassionate, kind, and curious. You are not bad, bad things happened to you. The blame and shame do not belong to you even if your body responded to the sexual stimuli. I will be a safe person for you to talk to."

Together we will:

"Acknowledge and face the truth of what happened, normalize that bad things happen to good people and innocent children, but it doesn't make you bad. We will not demonize or shame ourselves because it isn't helpful. I don't want you to be stuck here. You deserve more than that. Some bad things happened to you, or maybe you did some bad things, but that does not mean there is something wrong with you or that you are bad."

Only surviving:

"Yes, I want you to survive, and I want you to celebrate that you have survived. Look at you, you are smart and innovative and creative. Surviving is wonderful, but I want more for you because I don't want you stuck in survival mode. It was necessary for a time, but you were never meant to live in survival mode. It is exhausting, and it will affect your long-term health. You deserve better than that."

Transformation:

"I want you to be transformed. I want you to experience yourself in a new light. I want freedom and joy for you. Rewrite your story from darkness to light, hopeless to hopeful, from fear to faith. I want your story to include freedom and joy. I want your sexuality to be a delightful part of who you are as a woman. And remember, you can't do this alone. You need other safe people to help you heal. Part of your healing is learning it is okay to ask for help."

God designed you to overcome. As He encouraged the Shulamite to dance her dance of victory, so He wants you to dance in victory. However, there is one thing that will stop this dance—shame. Shame says you are bad, less than, dirty, never enough, responsible, and convictable. It has nothing helpful to add, and this critical judge can become the loudest voice in our heads. But it's time we push back by saying to that critical inner voice, "If you would like to say that in a kinder way I will have this conversation with you; if not this conversation is over."

If you cannot find a kind voice, then borrow someone's voice who is kind, warm, and nurturing. Practice using that voice when you talk to yourself, and hear that voice in your head, while you learn to speak to yourself with kindness and compassion. Most of us say 1000 mean things to ourselves a day, so it's no wonder we struggle with feeling unloved when our inner voice is so cruel.

Over the years and decades, God has brought me to the truth that He fashioned me with love and deliberation. There was nothing haphazard about how God made me, it was significantly more special and set apart than I could fathom. As females, we are the crown of God's creation. As I have embraced this truth in my life, it has liberated me from feeling badly about myself or not enjoying my body because of shame messages. Now, I feel curious and creative about my body, and I appreciate it. God knew we women would need some extra special messages and He gave those to us through the design of our bodies, we just haven't been taught them or known how to tune into them.

CHAPTER THREE

FEMALE SEXUAL ANATOMY

God is a creative genius, and he took profound intentionality in the formation of female sexuality. The only function of the clitoris is pleasure, while the penis is multi-functional. God purposely gave women an organ specifically designed for sexual pleasure. That is its one and only purpose. God is clearly stating that female sexual pleasure is of value to Him, and if that is true then it debunks the idea that female sexuality was created solely to dutifully serve male sexuality.

"The clitoris is as crucial to female sexuality as the penis is to a male. The clitoris and penis are somewhat mirror images of each other, just organized differently. MRI studies reveal that the clitoris is actually a complex, powerful organ system composed of a total of eighteen parts, two thirds of which are interior."[i]

Connected to the glans by the internal corpora cavernosa, are two spongy areas of erectile tissue. The corpora cavernosa branches off further down into a pair of wings known as the crura which extend into the body and around the vaginal canal like a wishbone. "Underneath the crura are the clitoral vestibules, or vestibular bulbs. Like much of the clitoris, these sac-like structures of tissue become engorged with blood when a female is aroused." [ii]

The clitoris is the most nerve-rich part of the vulva containing about 8,000 nerve endings making it the live wire of pleasure. To get some perspective, that's double the amount of nerve endings as the penis. And it gets even better, this erogenous zone spreads pleasure to 15,000 other nerves in the pelvis region. This is why it feels like your whole body is being taken over during sexual arousal and orgasm.

When the brain turns off, sexual turn-on begins. Only when the amygdala—the fear and anxiety center of the brain—has been deactivated can impulses rush to the pleasure centers and trigger an orgasm. Worry, fear, shame, work, kids, stress, or household responsibilities can interrupt the dance toward orgasm.

The need to turn off the brain explains why it takes a woman, on average, three to ten times longer than her husband to reach climax.

"It's a delicate dance, but the connection to the brain is about as direct as it gets. Nerves in the clitoris communicate straight to the sexual pleasure center of the female brain. When those nerves are stimulated, they boost electrochemical activity until it hits a threshold, triggers a burst of impulses, and releases bonding, feel-good neurochemicals such as dopamine, oxytocin, and endorphins."

If clitoral stimulation is cut off too soon (this is why a woman loves a *slow* steady hand), or if shame, guilt, fear, or stress overtakes her brain then the march toward climax is stopped dead in its tracks.

A woman needs to feel relaxed, comfortable, warm, and cozy to have good sex. The need to snuggle and cuddle up to her husband with kissing and caressing for her brain to become calm and the areas for genital and breast sensitivity to light up is real. It takes time, and as he begins to touch her clitoris, her brain can begin to spark red, and her amygdala will deactivate into a calm blue. "As she becomes more excited and invites him inside of her, the amygdala will completely deactivate, and the pleasure centers will pulse red, until rapid waves of orgasm flood her brain and body."[iii]

A woman needs to be put in the mood before sex. She needs a soothing and smoothing of the relationship. Anger at one's partner is one of the most common causes of sexual problems. Foreplay doesn't start in bed, it's everything that has happened in the 24 hours before sex.

She needs to reconnect positively with her partner to get in the mood. So yes husbands, wine her and dine her and befriend her before you attempt to recline her.

CHAPTER FOUR

LIBERATING VIEW OF SEXUALITY

I want everyone to have a liberating view of sexuality instead of a liberal view. A liberal view sounds like, "I can have sex with whomever I want, whenever I want and there are no confines to my sexuality because it is boundaryless and purposeless," but I don't think this is liberating or loving at all.

We have been taught that sex is just sex, but if that were true, why would God have gone through so much trouble just for humans to have a 30 second orgasm? Sex is about love, bonding, connection, attachment, and the mysterious feelings that pass between a husband and wife. We need to attach more value on sex, not less, and we need to take it more thoughtfully and attempt to understand all that God was trying to communicate when He made us sexual creatures.

When we think about sex, we are thinking about sexual behaviors such as intercourse, but when we talk about sexuality we are talking about our personhood, which is a bigger picture than sexual acts. Our sexuality gives us drive, energy, desire, and passion for life. Our sexuality causes us to long for romantic relationships. God separated woman from man so they could feel that longing.

God created us with a deep sexual longing to be one again and making love is the way we do that. We make love by bringing all of our sexuality to the bed, all of our personhood. We are not just coming to have sex. We are eye to eye, body to body, and heart to heart—an intermingling of our hearts and souls. Just like the beginning when male and female were encapsulated into one another.

In Galatians 5:1 it says that it is for freedom we have been saved, and honestly, human sexuality needs to be saved. Our sexuality needs a total transformation. Scripture says Satan has a particular hatred for women. Our bodies are so incredible, and I think there is jealousy. At a young age, Satan starts saying to us, "You are not enough. You're not pretty enough or as talented as someone else." Then we compete for male attention and allow others to define us: mothers, fathers, boyfriends, husbands. None of that is healthy. God alone wants to define us. If we allow God to do His work in our sexuality we would be transformed as women and we would show up in the world in a much different way. We would own our beauty, power, and strength, and make this world a better, more loving place.

CHAPTER FIVE

SEXUAL HISTORY

Every woman has a sexual history, and every woman can carry false guilt about her sexuality or shame about herself as a sexual creature. Sometimes, just the topic of sexuality can put our nervous systems on high alert, depending on how we were raised and our early experiences. However, I would like to help you uncover your story.

Stories are truly a powerful thing and when we can tell our story and bring our secrets into the light, we can rewrite our ending. I want to give you permission to not only tell your story, unearth your past, and grieve your losses, but also to discover, claim, and own the full- ness of the unique expression of your sexual self.

It may surprise you to know women are as sexual as men; they just have a different pathway for getting there. Female sexuality looks different from male sexuality and there is no shame in that. We will never get to the fun part of discovering our sexual selves if we are buried under shame, self-hatred, and secrets. Secrets are suffocating to their keepers, and the only way to begin a true sexual journey of freedom is to unearth that which is hidden.

In order to be healthy sexually, we have to be committed to the personal growth process, which in truth is a journey that begins in the form of story, your story. It doesn't matter where you are or what you have experienced—it matters where you are going.

If you choose to move toward embracing your healthy sexual self, understand this is not a "take a few numbered steps and you're done" process. No, this truly is a journey. But like any journey, you have to start somewhere, so start with you. Start by being honest with yourself about your sexual past and give yourself permission not to minimize your experiences and the affect your history has had on you. It was never God's intent for us to do life alone. Your personal growth process requires courage. But know it's okay to ask for help and even to need help.

Sadly, people can do some pretty cruel things to one another. Jesus came to this earth to heal the brokenhearted and to set the captives free (Isaiah 61). He is near the hurting and promises to never leave you. He brings comfort to those who grieve. Let Him draw near to you right now. He is not ashamed of you or your story.

God says in His word that bad things will happen because we live in a fallen, broken world. Too often we blame Him for those bad things, when in reality it is humans who make the hurtful choices. He loves you, is for you, gave up His Son for your healing, and sent the comforter, the Holy Spirit, to be with you. He will never ask you to do something and then leave you alone to do it. If you invite Him to join you on this journey, He happily will.

CHAPTER SIX

SEXUALITY FOR SINGLES

I t's silly to think that because you are single you are any less or any more sexual than a married person. God made you a sexual creature on purpose and with a plan in mind. It isn't a cosmic mistake that is meant to be a curse to you. Sexuality is a powerful gift, when stewarded well.

So, what do you do with your sexual urges and surges? Our culture says, "Do anything you want, when you want, how you want, and with whom you want." Yet, we see the consequences of this thinking everywhere we look. Millions of Americans live with an STI and a broken heart.

Some of you have experienced sexual harassment and sexual abuses. If I could sit with you and hear your story, you may tell me about how your heart was broken by sexual decisions. Maybe you have experienced someone taking from you sexually. Maybe you gave yourself to someone who you thought would love you forever. Maybe you hoped if you gave yourself to someone they would value you more. Perhaps you have used your sexuality to prove something to someone. Misuses of sexuality are a human condition. The Bible is full of stories of saints who have misused this gift. But again, God made you a sexual creature on purpose; it is a gift to be stewarded well.

Start by acknowledging your sexual urges and celebrate that everything is working the way God intended it to. Don't repress your sexual feelings. When you repress them, they have a way of sneaking out of you in ways that can surprise and shock you. Instead, acknowledge them so you can thank God everything is working and then you can let them go and move on. Go work out, connect with friends and family, create meaningful non-sexual relationships. Have non-sexual affection met non-sexually. You need hugs and warm embraces.

Your sexual desires have a deeper purpose. God gave us sexual desire to draw us towards a future spouse. If we didn't have desire, we wouldn't marry and we wouldn't make babies together. The world, as we know it, would cease. Sexual desire is meant to pull you towards someone so you can get to know them and possibly fall in love.

Intimacy begins with friendship, exploring if you would be good together. The problem with hopping in bed with each other is then sex becomes the focus instead of cultivating a deep friendship and discovering the depths of this other person's personality, spirituality, and character. Listen, sex is great, and I get that many of you want to have sex. I think that's a good thing, but it needs to be in the right context to be the liberating type of sex God made you for.

I don't think God is a sexual prude. Quite the opposite. He is the one who created erogenous zones and decided to give males a penis that fits into a vagina and gave hundreds of pleasurable nerve endings to enjoy sexual union. He gave curves to women with breasts and hips and other pretty parts. He gave men equal but different beauty. He isn't a prude; He is a protector.

God teaches us to protect our hearts, and marriage was meant to provide a safe context where you are loved and cherished, and you have a solid covenant to hold you together in good and bad times. This covenant was intended for you to feel safe and trusting. Trust is the ability to be careless. In this context, you can let go sexually, explore, play, and feast with one another as you learn how to make love together.

Forgive us married people for not presenting a great picture of married sex. We have failed our single friends. I want you to know that marriage can be a delight.

Married sex can be a feast. Maybe you love being single, and I want to echo what the Apostle Paul advocated when he said, "I wish you all were single like me." But, if you have an ache for a companion, don't wait for him to magically show up. Go out and find him.

Pursue what your heart aches for. But, in the process, steward this beautiful, valuable part of yourself. You may have already had sex, maybe lots of sex with lots of different partners. Ask God to forgive you for treating your body, and perhaps other people's bodies, with little regard. Put support around yourself, and pursue the kind of sexual relationship that will fill you up, instead of leaving you more empty than before you had sex.

As a church we have done a bad job of honoring and celebrating single sexuality. The apostle Paul said it's great to marry but even better to be single because you have more time for the kingdom of God and to focus on His purposes. You also have more time for many deep relationships and to pursue what God has called you to do. If you have been called to celibacy, recognize your body still has pleasurable sexual feelings and acknowledge that means you are human.

Marriage is holy, but there is something equally holy about singleness, and if you have the gift of celibacy it is a beautiful thing. Be proud and enjoy it. You are much more like the Apostle Paul than I, so celebrate your wholeness. You are not any less sexual because you aren't married, in the same way you aren't any more of a sexual creature because you are married. Marriage simply means you have a sexual partner, but you are still who God made you—a sexual creature. So be at peace with whatever that looks like for you.

Letter to my single daughters

My Beautiful Daughter:

I want you to know your value, your worth, your incredible beauty, dignity, and how your sexuality is integrated into every one of those pieces. I hope you will hold onto these truths because they will be protective. I'm not saying we can prevent all the sexual ills of the world by having a higher degree of value for yourself and others, but I believe there is something about the way a woman carries herself that communicates a lot.

I believe most of the world is filled with good humans; but there are also predators out there. If I were to line up 100 men and women, a percentage of them will be predators, so I don't want you going into the world naively. Nor do I want you feeling like you can't trust anyone. Be wise, listen to your gut and keep safe friends around you and be aware of the role alcohol plays in sexual assaults and in regret sex.

I understand sexual mistakes, I have made them and so have most others, so there is no condemnation, judgment, or shame. But I want you to be with males who are worthy of you, not just males looking for sexual satisfaction. That is usury and your life has more value than that, as does your body.

I want you to go with your values in place because God has a great plan for your sexuality. God is the One who invented sex, attraction, hormones, and arousal. He could have made us mechanical like cars, but He didn't. Instead, He created us with sexual mystery, and I hope you will hold this gift as a mystery as you seek to understand it.

CHAPTER SEVEN

SEXUALITY FOR MARRIED WOMEN

Some believe sexuality was the devil's idea. I understand that thinking, given the horrendous ways we humans have used sexuality to manipulate, shame, control, harm, and overpower others. But clearly, sexuality was introduced before the fall of mankind and our God is *the* God of Love. Simply stated, He is Love. He loves the world. And He invites us to love one another, saying it is the greatest thing we'll ever do. We are to love others as we love ourselves.

A relationship not growing in love will not be secure and solid. Love is a must. His word begins with a marriage in Genesis and finishes in grand finale with a marriage in Revelation, supporting the idea God made us for love relationships. God is in a sweet community of love, and He invites us to create and participate with Him in loving relationships.

Our sexuality is intended to be grounded and rooted in God's love. He created mankind as one human being and then extracted the feminine from the masculine. They were originally one, and sexual intercourse is the way in which the two become one again. God created sexual longing when He separated the two; instinctively, they long for the familiarity of the other's body and desire one another sexually. That God-given desire is a part of our makeup.

Letter to My Married Daughters

My Beautiful Daughters:

I am thrilled for you to be entering into marriage. There is nothing more divine than laying naked in the arms of the man you love while making love to each other. The sweetness that is meant to be shared in the marriage bed is one of the most exquisite experiences of a lifetime. You will be an important part of creating and forming something sweet and good between you both.

Remember, he is not in your body and can't feel what you are feeling. Only you can feel what you are feeling. It is important for you to use your voice and teach him how to touch you and how to make love to you. You are the only one who can teach him what is good and right for you.

There may be times when you feel you have it all figured out and that you've found your sexual rhythm, but then suddenly you are struggling with cramps, PMS, infertility, pregnancy, or menopause. A woman's body is mysterious, so allow your body to be mysterious. Be kind, compassionate, gentle, and patient with your body all the days of your life and it will bring you much satisfaction.

It takes a woman, on average, 21 minutes to become aroused. Yes, there are times when you will become aroused more quickly, but most times you will need more time and care. So don't be critical toward your body. Oftentimes a woman starts in a state of sexual neutrality, deciding if she is in the mood. This is okay, and this is why foreplay is coreplay. It takes a woman a while to warm up. Sometimes she doesn't know what she wants; she just needs to be willing. It is helpful for a husband to clearly express his sexual desire, which will help woo her into her own.

A woman doesn't always need an orgasm, nor does she always have the energy for one. She may just enjoy the closeness of making love. However, if a woman goes too long without having an orgasm, she begins to lose interest. Only 30% of females have an orgasm during intercourse. This is okay. It is important for you to teach your man how to touch you sexually and for you both to slow down, allowing enough time for the clitoris and the entire vulva region to become fully aroused. There are hundreds of erogenous zones on the female body. So give yourselves time to build arousal and be curious about your body. Sexuality is meant to be a mystery, and you my darling are mysterious.

While pleasuring him is important, don't rush it. He will delight in learning how to pleasure you and you will delight in his pleasure. His pleasure is oftentimes far more instantaneous. Teach your man how to please you and give yourself the time you need to become aroused and then focus on his pleasure as well as your own. Females aren't good at receiving because we are trained to constantly give; however, the bedroom is the best place to practice receiving. Lay back, relax, breathe deeply, and let him pleasure you; and if he isn't great at it then kindly teach him how.

Wait to have intercourse until you are wanting him to enter you. Females are multi-orgasmic; pay attention to those little quivers that are oftentimes the gentle side of an orgasm. Take the time to notice those little quivers, you may be multi-orgasmic, but you just haven't noticed. Soak in those quivers and make time for the grand finale. Learn the language of your body.

Have a lot of grace and compassion for yourself because what might be arousing in one moment may not be in the next. Stay kind and compassionate towards your body and always be curious. Let there be time for the two of you to practice making love to each other. Understand you don't need to be the best at love making when you start, you have a lifetime to practice this magnificent gift God has given you. Let it unfold.

CHAPTER EIGHT

SEX: GOD'S IDEA

Biblical endorsement of female sexual desire and sexual longing is expressed best in the Song of Songs chapter 1:12–13. The Woman speaks: "When my King-Lover lay down beside me my fragrance filled the room. His head resting between my breasts—the head of my lover was a sachet of sweet myrrh…Oh, let me warn you, sisters in Jerusalem, by the gazelles, yes, by all of the wild deer. Don't excite love, don't stir it up, until the time is ripe—and you're ready." (Is she advocating for women to be fully aroused before they have intercourse, which would help alleviate pain and help females become more orgasmic?)

The Man speaks: "I went to my garden, dear friend, best lover! Breathed the sweet fragrance. I ate the fruit and honey. I drank the nectar and wine." (Song of Songs 5:1,5,13, MSG). He continually refers to her as his dearest friend and best lover. Sexuality is always about mutuality. 1 Corinthians 7:2–3 says it like this: "Is it a good thing to have sexual relations? Certainly—but only within a certain context. It's good for a man to have a wife, and for a woman to have a husband. Sexual drives are strong, but marriage is strong enough to contain them and provide for a balanced and fulfilling sexual life in a world of sexual disorder. The Marriage bed must be a place of mutuality—the husband seeking to satisfy his wife, the wife seeking to satisfy her husband. Marriage is not a place to 'stand up for your rights.'"

Marriage is a decision to love the other, whether in bed or out. Being sexual with another human was intended to be an expression of a love relationship.

Scripture clearly makes a connection between married love and sex—a very necessary connection to make if we are going to reclaim the meaning and purpose of our sexuality. Some eliminate sex when they talk about love, thinking sexuality isn't holy enough to be connected to love, and others eliminate love when they talk about sex, believing sex is about lust.

God wants us to have an integrated *wholeness* as we develop our ideas, thinking, and beliefs about human sexuality. He wants us to have a love map for the expression of our sexuality. Sexuality is a significant part of our story, and our parents play a role in how we feel about our sexuality and what we do with it. If our parents had a healthy view of sexuality and were comfortable talking about sex, that shaped us in a positive way. If they were unhealthy and sex was a taboo topic in the house you grew up in, sex can be a really difficult topic.

If sex was treated without respect, such as if porn was readily available, or off-handed sexual innuendos were tossed around, or parents were sexually unfaithful to one another, sexuality can seem dirty. If Mom and Dad modeled warmth, affection, and playful attraction, we learned our sexuality is something good. If our parents argued about sex, if one was cold and the other pouted because sex wasn't frequent enough, we learn sex is a power struggle. Either way, our parents helped wire our brains for future sexual relationships.

You may feel discouraged by this. Ron and I were at first as well. Neither set of our parents modeled healthy sexuality. There were lots of dark secrets to be sorted through. With God's help and the help of others, we can honestly say no sexual problem, no shameful secret, nothing you are hiding from is too impossible for God to heal. God created your sexuality for a purpose, but you may wonder why.

Why, God, when it can be so destructive? The reason sex is often so hurtful is because it is powerful. Sex is a metaphor for a God who wants an intimate, knowing relationship with each one of His children. Think how the enemy must hate this intimate part of

God's purpose and how he wants to bring destruction to our sexuality. Your sexual history is a part of who you are. Instead of fearing it, be honest with yourself about your experiences, both positive and negative, and how those experiences have shaped and impacted you. Find safe relationships to sort it through, and ask for help if you need it. Your sexual wholeness is worth reclaiming.

We have to remember sex is God's idea. His intention was for sex to bond a man and woman to one another in a covenantal relationship—a relationship that provides sexual safety. He never intended for sex to be used as a weapon of violence, or dominance, or anger, or hurt. I am sure God grieves deeply for what we humans have done with this most exquisite of gifts and for what you women have been through. Again, He never intended for us to have experienced sexual trauma.

CHAPTER NINE

FEELING SAFE

The female brain has to feel safe in order for her to relax enough to enjoy sex. Think about it: females are more vulnerable than males when it comes to sex. Men are stronger and bigger, and that fact alone can feel physically threatening to a woman. She can fear getting pregnant, knowing that a pregnancy requires so much more from her than it does her male partner. She also knows her path to sensuality is slower than her husband's. Females need much more emotional connection, talking, caressing, and time to get into desire and arousal than men typically do.

The woman in the Song of Songs goes on to say, "Rise up, south wind! Blow on my garden" (NLT). The south wind is warm and inviting. She wants to warm up and get things enlivened in her garden, which is a reference to her vulva. She wants to experience sexual desire and to feel the wetness of arousal and the fragrance that is released from a woman's body when she is sexually ready. This sounds like a reference to intercourse and perhaps oral sex and the many delectable ways they enjoy her garden together. And this is all possible when her brain and her body work together, in a safe context. God made sex for pleasure and attachment, as well as for reproducing offspring. He made it possible for couples to enjoy many varieties of sexual pleasure, from a foot rub and body massage, to discovering the over three hundred erogenous zones on a woman's body, kissing, caressing, breast stimulation, manual and oral play, and intercourse.

God is a creative artist and when it comes to human sexuality, I think He wants us to be creative and imaginative. Sex between a husband and wife is completely *unique* to that couple. Every couple has the right to figure out what they consider pleasurable and take into consideration one another's personal preferences. No one should force or pressure another person into anything. It's important we hear one another's 'No!' and respect it. When choice is absent so is love. It's also important that we stay open and communicative. It is normal for humans to desire sex; there's nothing wrong with that as long as mutuality and love are the values we cling to.

Sex is a beautiful way to bridge an attachment breach when you have missed an attachment *cue* from your spouse. The comfort and warmth of your partner's skin on your skin can soothe the pain of separation. Many times, if sex is about connection and expressing love, bodies can repair and make up faster than our brains can. Powerful feel-good hormones are released when a man and a woman go chest to chest, belly to belly, skin on skin. Caressing, kissing, and touching sensitive erogenous zones helps you get out of your head and into your body. Sometimes a couple just needs to put their annoyances or frustrations on the shelf and make love to each other.

I believe God thinks it is great when we try to make love to our partner even if fireworks don't go off—cuddling, playing, and fondling are all good. We need to take the focus off of having intercourse and an orgasm and put the value on giving each other pleasure. Pleasure is underrated. Pleasure for your body and giving your spouse pleasure is worthy of our time and effort. God wants you to have the feel-good hormones released in your body to make marriage easier. It's like a free mini-vacation—why wouldn't you go?

It's so easy to judge a man and think all he wants is sex; or the other extreme, he never wants me anymore. Get into your own solid self and pursue him sexually. Men want to be wanted as much as a woman wants to be wanted. No one wants to be judged for his or her sexual desires or lack of desire. If you don't want him pawing at you then give him reassurance that he is desirable by pursuing him.

CHAPTER TEN

UNDERSTANDING FEMALE AND MALE SEXUAL DIFFERENCES

The sexual desire hormone for both males and females is the androgen testosterone, this hormone is mistakenly called the 'male' hormone. The truth is, it's actually a sex and aggression hormone, and both males and females have plenty of it" (Brizendine, Louann. *The Female Brain*). The male body makes it in their testes and adrenal glands, while females produce it in their ovaries and adrenal glands. Testosterone is the hormonal fuel that gets the brain's sexual engine revving.

"When there's enough fuel, testosterone revs the hypothalamus, igniting erotic feelings and arousing sexual fantasies and physical sensations in the erogenous zones. The process works the same for both men and women, but there is a huge difference in the amount of testosterone available. On average, men have ten to one hundred times more testosterone than women" (Brizendine, Louann. *The Female Brain*).

Because of this higher dose of jet fuel, men normally have three times more sex drive than women. And if a woman's limited testosterone levels drop, she'll completely lose interest. (Have your hormones checked if you have lost interest. There are bioidentical hormones available, which are safer than the formerly used synthetic ones.) Parallel structures in the sex-related centers of the male brain are about two times bigger than the same structure in the female brain.

Male and female brains are 99.9% alike, but the 0.1% makes a huge difference in the way we think, feel, and respond to sex. "Men literally have sex on their brains more than women do. They have double the brain space and processing power devoted to sex as females. Just like women have an eight-lane superhighway for processing emotions, while men have a meandering country road, men have O'Hare Airport as a hub for processing thoughts about sex, whereas women have the airfield nearby that lands small planes and personal jets" (Brizendine, Louann. *The Female Brain*).

What females don't understand about men is what sex means to them. Men have been judged unfairly when a woman says, "all he wants is sex." It may feel that way, but sex has meaning for him. Typically, women need to be more sympathetic to what sex means to her husband. When a wife is too tired for sex or doesn't want to engage sexually with him, he can feel like she doesn't want him anymore, or worse, she doesn't love him. Her lack of desire can send him into depression. "This is like what happens with a woman and verbal communication. If her husband stops talking to her or responding emotionally, she thinks he disapproves of her, that she has done something wrong, or he doesn't love her anymore. She'll panic that she's losing him" (Brizendine, Louann. *The Female Brain*).

A woman needs to have compassion for how her husband is wired sexually. She needs to understand God made his sexual center two times larger than the same structure in her brain. Men need to understand that she needs more warm-up time with conversations, kisses, caresses and help with the kids and housework. Being generous and moving outside of our natural comfort zones are a must for marriages to maintain a fulfilling sexual relationship.

CHAPTER ELEVEN

SEX IS HER CHOICE

The brain is the female's most important sex organ. Whatever you are saying to yourself about this man of yours will translate directly into how you feel sexually about him and yourself. In the Song of Songs when the Shulamite is talking about how he lays his head between her breasts, she just breathes him in and recalls the beautiful love they make together. She isn't focusing on how he leaves his dirty clothes on the floor or the bodily noises he seems to enjoy making. No, is she focused on how he makes her body feel and the amazing things he does to her. It's a sensual feast. She engaged her sense of smell and taste, and what she hears and sees, which ignites her sexually.

Make it fun. Make it interesting. Get into it. Use lubrication. Don't lie there and expect him to turn you on. You get into it. Help him get you ready to receive him. Be an active lover. Kiss him passionately and deeply. Play with his body, and invite him to play with yours. Ask him to touch you in your favorite ways. Don't hold back. Sex is so good for you.

I can't tell you the women I have had in my office who say, "I never have an orgasm anymore and sex sort of hurts or is uncomfortable." I ask them, "How long are you giving yourself to get aroused? Are you enjoying ten to twenty-one minutes of foreplay?"

"Well, no. It's all pretty fast." If that's your answer as well, then you and your husband aren't having mutually pleasurable sex. You are probably servicing him.

Listen, I think a husband and a wife owe each other sex. (Unless there is abuse or pain. If there is abuse please seek immediate help. If you are having pelvic floor pain, please see a pelvic floor specialist.) When you said, "I do," you were promising to be this person's forever sexual partner, to the best of your ability. I get sickness, kids, surgery, and other circumstances that cause sexual pauses. But we can't stay there. Here's the thing: I don't believe in duty sex.

Ultimately, duty sex or servicing your man sexually ends up being pretty empty and eventually a resentment-building experience for both the husband and the wife. Typically, the belief behind duty sex is, "He needs it and if I don't give it to him at least occasionally he will be tempted, and I don't want him cheating." If that is your belief system, that doesn't come from a place of love and redemption, that comes from a place of fear.

Deal with the fear so you can truly make love to the man you said, "I do," to. The men I have asked how duty sex feels for them say this, "It's not what I want. It does the job, but I wish she wanted me, and I wish I wasn't another chore for her to check off the list." Ouch!

Can you hear his hurt? Men are far more tender than they let us in on. I don't think this is what God wants for any marriage. I mentioned 1 Corinthians before, but I want to repeat what the Apostle Paul said: "It's good for a man to have a wife, and for a woman to have a husband. Sexual drives are strong, but marriage is strong enough to contain them and provide for a balanced and fulfilling sexual life in a world of sexual disorder. The marriage bed MUST be a place of mutuality—the husband seeking to satisfy his wife, the wife seeking to satisfy her husband. Marriage is a decision to serve the other, whether in bed or out" (1 Corinthians 7:3–5, MSG).

Paul makes a great point here; marriage is the willingness to serve another. I think we can serve each other, and sex is the most fulfilling when the husband wants to give his wife pleasure and she wants to give him pleasure. Take pleasure in your spouse's pleasure and you double the pleasure. Paul also affirms that sexual drives are strong. You have complete biblical support to have strong sexual drives. The only caveat is to put those strong sexual urges in the right context: marriage.

Women don't compare yourselves to your husbands. Most likely, especially when he's young, his erections are pretty instant and spontaneous. All he needs is to see you or think about sex and the rocket is ready to launch. Women are just as sexual, but need more warm-up time and some inviting to get into their bodies. Men actually become more like females sexually as they age and testosterone levels lower. It can be kind of great because then he needs more play time too.

Dr. Rosemary Basson helps us have a better understanding of female sexuality when she says, "After having children or after being in a relationship for several years, sex becomes more of a choice for a woman, she slips more into sexual neutrality." What she is saying is that earlier in the relationship you may have had lots of hot passion for your man, then your jets cooled as the years went on.

I noticed when this changed for me. It was between the birth of our second and third son. We had been married for a while, and we were deep into baby land. I thought to myself while vacuuming the family room and holding a baby on my hip, *hmmm, where did my Oh La La go? I miss that.* What I did notice was that even though I may not have that powerful *Oh La La* of desire, if I engaged with Ron sexually, after a while, I would move from sexually neutral to finding a willingness to engage, to finding first gear, then the second, the third, and we were off to the races. It just took a little longer, but it was still there if I would just remind myself how great it is once I get into it.

I think too many women shut down the idea when their husband initiates because she isn't in the mood right then and there. You may not be, but I want to encourage you to engage and go for it, knowing it will come. Give it time; wait for it. It's always worth it. I frequently ask women, "When you do engage sexually with your man are you glad you did in the end?" Do you ever hear yourself saying, "We should do that more often"? That's because you are sexual and when you are married, the Apostle Paul, the single guy, says to have sex frequently; it's super good for you.

Married couples who have sex regularly live longer, have better heart health, enjoy a deeper connection, and can let go of annoyances easier. I'm sure someday in heaven, God will give us a million more reasons why He made sex for husband and wife to enjoy and why it was so good for us.

So here is my encouragement to you: Do it. Do it often, as often as is fun. Push yourself a little. Get your groove on. Find your mojo. Give it your best and your all. Be courageous. Go for it. Seriously, your marriage will be more fun, richer, deeper, sexier, much more connected if you do. It's the only thing you have that is all yours. It has the potential to be a sweet part of your marriage. Make out on the couch, in the shower, in the car. Be sexual with each other. Make it all it can be.

Don't let this beautiful thing God made die. That's a sad, long, painful death. Fight for it. Don't give up on it. Don't be passive or aggressive about it. Do whatever you have to do to make this work for you both. Talk. Become sexual friends. Turn him on. Let yourself get turned on. Be willing and get help if you are completely stuck. There is no shame in needing help; the shame is if you need help and don't have the courage to ask for it.

Shame harasses us with the endless questions: what is wrong with you? This is torment. If we don't acknowledge what shame does to all of us, then we will continue to be tormented by it. And this is not the life God wants us to live. God invites us to come home to love. Christ is inviting you to come home—right here—He is the Christ within. Christ indwells you. He is love, and so He is wooing you to come home to love.

God created sexuality to be a beautiful expression of our love for another human. There is absolutely nothing dirty, shameful, or despicable about a loving husband and wife making love to each other. It is good, and it is to be celebrated and enjoyed.

Unless it isn't . . .

I knew a beautiful Christian couple where married sex became dirty, shameful, and despicable. He was bored with their sex life, or so he said, when really he was trying to avoid the sadness and depression in his own soul. And so he invited others into their bed: porn, prostitutes, and people to share their marriage bed—and she complied. Illicit sex is a dangerous slippery slope and in the end their marriage was in a heap at the bottom, destroyed. This is why scripture says the marriage bed is sacred, "Honor marriage, and guard the sacredness of sexual intimacy between wife and husband. God draws a firm line against casual and illicit sex" (Hebrews 13:4, MSG).

Married sex is sacred. Your body, his body, is sacred. Be respectful, loving, kind, warm, and nurturing towards each other. See your bodies as a gift made by God for God. See him as a gift, a gift God has entrusted to you. Be wise with these gifts, and make repairs if you have been unkind, neglectful, or foolish. Acknowledge damage done. Trust God is still bigger than any mistakes you or he have made, and realize you are too valuable to keep repeating the same mistakes.

No matter what sexual mistakes have been made, God is not ashamed of you. If the stories in the Bible are true, then it's clear He knew we would make lots of mistakes, and yet not once does He turn His back on us; instead He gave His son to cover every mistake we've ever made. Lay down your sexual shame and invite God to cleanse and redeem the sexual parts of you. Start over, at the very beginning, and let Him rewrite your sexual narratives.

CHAPTER TWELVE

HAPPY MARRIED SEX

Not every married couple has happy sex. Some couples are shy and awkward with one another. Some were raised in homes where they were taught sexual feelings are shameful and even disgusting. For others, he or she brings sexual baggage into the marriage and that baggage becomes a wall—prohibiting sexual enjoyment. I think some folks are just more selfish by nature and haven't learned how to share their bodies with their spouse.

As Eugene Peterson so beautifully stated in his introduction to the Song of Songs, "The Song makes a connection between love and sex—a very important and very biblical connection to make. There are some who would eliminate sex when they speak of love, supposing that they are making it more holy. Others, when they think of sex, never think of love. The Song proclaims an integrated wholeness that is at the center of Christian teaching on committed, wedded love for a world that seems to specialize in loveless sex."[iv]

There are also situations where sex has become painful and downright horrible. If a man uses his power to force his wife to have sex or perform sexual acts against her will, well . . . no one wants to be treated like a sexual slave. If one partner has cheated or has a porn problem, this kills sexual desire for their partner as does being critical or complaining. If there has been selfish taking instead of generous sharing, this also destroys love—as does withholding from one another.

So, how do we heal when these things have happened? I would say, no probably shout, get help! Don't wait and hope, and then hope some more that things will magically change. Most likely they won't unless you get help. Seek out a professional, find a wise mentor, seek godly counsel, but stop trying to fix this on your own. The problem is bigger than the two of you.

If sex is boring, decide you will be the one to bring the fun! Start by thinking about the last sexual encounter you had with your husband that was good, connecting, warm, and loving. Think about how it felt to have his body next to yours and take in the memory of how bonding it felt to be with him. Now, think of something new you could bring to the bed. Something fun to wear? A new perfume, candle, or light for the room? Take a shower and put your hair up, spray perfume on and then come to bed with a message that says, "I want you and I am here to play with you."

Attitude is everything, and what you say to yourself about your spouse and yourself matters. If you are obsessing over all of the ways he disappoints you, he will sense it. Neuroscience teaches that whatever we focus on grows. Do you want to grow your respect and affection for him? Then remind yourself of all of the ways you do love and respect him. Surely, you can find a few things you like about him. After all, you picked him, and you could have chosen not to. You wanted to spend the rest of your life with him. So love him and love him well. Sex for married women largely becomes a choice. Quit waiting for the Oh-La-La sexual feelings. Instead, cultivate them. Once you remember the sexual creature God made you to be and engage, wow, it's fun and bonding and good. An orgasm is super good for you and releases all kinds of feel good hormones that bond you to your man more deeply and soothe some of the annoyances of being married.

You have to be open to teaching your spouse how to make love to you. You have to talk to him. What turned you on last week may not this week. He doesn't know unless you talk to him. But talk to him kindly. Say what you mean, but don't *say it mean.*

Don't be mean to him. Men are actually pretty sensitive on the inside and need some compassion just like we do. Put your hand over his and show him what you like. Or demonstrate for him what you like. He will most likely really appreciate you teaching him unless he has some other personality issues. I would also encourage you to tune into his body. We can treat men like they are sexual machines, they aren't. They have sexual likes and dislikes, preferences and even things that trigger them in a way that isn't arousing. Make it safe for him to talk with you about what he likes and what he doesn't like. Be his sexual friend and companion. Understand his sexual needs without judging him. Sexual intimacy means more to your man than he knows how to put into words. It goes deep into his soul when you make love to him.

Neuroscience teaches us that the male brain is wired to be extremely visual. This wiring in the nucleus accumbens resides in the back of the brain. It controls things we don't consciously think about like digestion and breathing. Clinical studies teach us that this part of the brain lights up in a man when he sees a sexual image, like his wife getting out of the shower. When the nucleus accumbens lights up, he will most likely experience a primal, physical urge to sexually "consume" what he sees. In order for a woman to *compassionately understand* her husband, she must know that sex means so much more to him than that initial desire to "consume" what he sees. Men report that just having sex isn't enough—it isn't satisfying unless their wives want them as well.

The females' sexual pathway is more leisurely than the speedway of male sexual desire. When a woman sees an attractive male, the nucleus accumbens typically stays dark, and instead, the cortical centers ignite and a woman thinks, *What a handsome man*—that's it. Women don't usually have an automatic sexual response like men do.

It is important to understand that men and women are wired sexually very differently. God did this on purpose—it's part of His design and plan. Let's celebrate those differences and make room for them. Let's let one another off the hook and begin to really enjoy one another. Sex is an important part of married life and God wants it to be a sweet and satisfying part of your marriage. He's inviting you to play in its waters, uninhibited. If that's not where you and your spouse find yourselves then sit down in a safe place (maybe a coffee shop), and talk about what you would like and then decide to pursue that together. Agree to not become defensive. Defensiveness kills a conversation. You may even start with prayer. Perhaps you've never asked God to enliven your sex life. Invite Him into the bedroom. This is His idea, after all. He will redeem it to be all He created and designed it to be. Sex is about intimacy—connection and pleasure—not just about the physical act.

For sex to become a loving, tender, mutual experience for the husband and the wife, we have to learn to understand our differences and keep the focus on connection and pleasure. Sex is more than skin on skin, more than intercourse and orgasm. Sex penetrates our souls and bonds us to one another. And what is needed is a healthy view of sex.

CHAPTER THIRTEEN

YOU ARE RESILIENT

This morning, as I gazed out the window, I watched as the black, inky sky turned to swirls of light blue and white. I noticed the trampoline my grandchildren love to jump wildly on, before throwing themselves into the pool, is now covered in white frost. Then my gaze traveled to the vine which faithfully climbs the arbor in my backyard. Surprised, I saw the three sunshine yellow blossoms clinging bravely to the vine, despite the cold. They are resilient, though they look delicate and fragile. Their resiliency delighted me because many other blossoms had fallen to the ground.

You are resilient. Resiliency is a needed requirement for this adult life. Resiliency is the ability to withstand, recover quickly from setbacks, spring back, adapt well to change, and to keep going. Life is best lived when we develop resiliency and when we stop treating ourselves as if we are fragile. You aren't fragile. You can recover from whatever life has thrown your way.

Your backbone is beautiful. Feel it strengthening, as you read this, and then face the sexual realities of your life. Reality is your best friend. Reality will help you grieve your sorrows, face your disappointments, and normalize that you are an imperfect human, as is the person you are married to. Grief helps us integrate the good and the bad, the happy and the sad, the strong feelings of love and passion, the realities of life, and the annoyances of relationships.

If you are married, there are most likely sexual conversations you need to have with your husband. Regulate your own emotions first. If you are emotionally unregulated, the conversation will not go well. Confront yourself, before you confront him. I have issues; you have issues; we all have issues, so take a good look at yourself, before you point your finger at him. Start softly; harshness never works. A soft start creates the possibility for a productive resolution.

Sexual issues are normal. Stop giving them so much power. You are competent to handle any of the hardships in your life. God promises not to give you more than you can bear up under. You are more resilient than you have thought you are. Every woman has the God-given right to enjoy the sex she is having. It takes courage to believe that and to stop sabotaging yourself.

If you are single, make sure you are treating your body as the gift it is, and only date those who will treat you with the same regard. When you value yourself, you see how shallow and meaningless the hookup culture is, and you believe you are worth more. You are worthy of love and dignity. If you treat yourself kindly, most likely so will others.

If you're married and sex is boring, painful, disconnected, unkind or extinct then decide that with God's help you are going to be the agent of change. You be the change you want to see. It's amazing how change in one person can change the dance you two have been doing. After all, God says, if He is for you then who can be against you; trust Him to help you be this agent of change. Surely the One who created you, as a sexual creature, is happy to partner with you in your pursuit of sexual joy, health, and happiness.

NOTES

[i] Nguyen JD, Duong H. <u>Anatomy, abdomen and pelvis, female external genitalia</u>. In: *StatPearls*.
StatPearls Publishing; 2022.

[ii] Nguyen JD, Duong H. <u>Anatomy, abdomen and pelvis, female external genitalia</u>. In: *StatPearls*. StatPearls Publishing; 2022.

[iii] Brizendine, Louann. *The Female Brain.* Bantam, 2009.

[iv] Peterson, Eugene H. *The Message.* NavPress, 2004.

[v] Rosemary Basson, "Rethinking Low Sexual Desire in Women," *BJOG: An International Journal of Obstetrics and Gynecology*, vol. 109, issue 4, April 2002: 357– 63, onlinelibrary.wiley.com.